God's Kingdom 1313

The Secret Pain

ISBN: 978-1-961879-10-2 (sc)
        978-1-961879-11-9 (e)

Publishing rev. date: 10/30/2023

God's Kingdom 1313

The Secret Pain

MARK-HOUR

Did you know you were *stolen* from your Heavenly Father?

How would knowledge of *you* being stolen from your heavenly Father, with you being infected with a *permanent emotional imbalance*, affect how you feel about your relationship with God now?

He came to what was his own, but his own people did not accept him.

John 1:11

To love and when rejected; learn to forgive, make new agreements, let go and move beyond.

And now these three remain: faith, hope, and love. But the greatest of these is love.

1 Corinthians 13:13

DEDICATION

This work is dedicated to my wife and children. I am truly sorry for all the emotional pain I have caused you through my selfish abandonment of your needs. I want so much for our complete healing that I hope through my own realization, practice and documentation of what I've learned, it will help others, too. In the end, good coming from bad; in unity with the Holy Spirit of God for the sake of each He calls to Himself.

May God continue to bless all those He wants me to pray for, those who He asks me to pray for and those who have no one to pray for them; especially the infirmed and dying. I also wish to thank every loving soul that has helped me throughout my life. Thanks also to God who is at work in every dear soul in prison—inmates, staff, and counselors alike. Thank you for allowing me the time to heal my mind.

TABLE OF CONTENTS

Dedication vii

Preface...xi

    Chapter One: Word..1

    Chapter Two: The Seven Swords of Sorrow 8

    Chapter Three: Root of Pain 14

    Chapter Four: Miss-Matched Expectations.........................23

    Chapter Five: Love Distorted by Fear and Pain..................34

    Chapter Six: What to Expect When You Go to Prison.....39

    Chapter Seven: Love Conquers Selfishness..........................48

    Chapter Eight: The Take Away..54

Further Reading 61

Acknowledgments 64

Written 03/17/2007

Eighteen months, eight days, five hours…and counting. What if this day was the last day you'd spend with your wife of six years, two-year-old daughter, and four-year-old son? What if you knew the prognosis was that you'd spend the next several years away from your family in prison? How would you spend your time? At home? On vacation?

My wife and I chose to spend our last meal together as a family as normal as possible in a restaurant. Bedtime was kept with me hugging and kissing my children good night, making an indistinguishable reference to my not being home for a long time, in reparation for a wrong that I had to make right. It was absolutely heart wrenching knowing that I would not be there for my family. Fear built up in me over the more than 15 months it took till sentencing. My lawyer said since I had confessed, there was truly nothing he could do to stop whatever would inevitably happen to me. Nerve racking does not even scratch the surface of the stress that builds in you and your loved ones toward your last moments as a family.

Walking from the peace of my home into the jowls of a courtroom is itself something I could write pages about but will rely on my reader to be vastly superior to my having to spell it all out. Try to remember your last, most painful separation. You know the one that caused *you* to be changed. If you've never had to endure a separation from loved ones, then imagine separating from the closest relationship you have now. Feel the anxiety and fear wash over your body as panic overcomes your sense of peace and well-being. Now imagine trying to pretend everything is normal while you spend the last months, then days, then hours, then minutes with those you live for and love most, as the inevitable separation presses on toward you facing your just due. How would you deal with it? Would you run away and hide? Would you turn yourself over, trusting in the balance of our justice system?

God's Kingdom 1313 The Secret Pain is about helping others navigate the pitfalls and consequences of rejection and emotional pain in *their* lives; increasing the depth of intimacy they feel in connection with God the Father and all souls. There may be times when you want to skip over some materials because it may seem too painful to you as you progress through it, and I ask that you allow it all to impact your conscious and subconscious alike. Each word was written, then refined over a period spanning 17 years. I am confident that you will benefit by it all; just be patient. Seemingly unimportant decisions can, and do have large ramifications for us all, in this life and that of the next.

It's now two hours and thirty-five minutes later than I began this work. I commit to keeping good company with you; Mark-Hour.

Note: The last 2 pages provide space to write your answers to my questions posed throughout the book.

Chapter One

Word

Emotional Pain: Human weakness or a pathway to empathy and self-fulfillment?

- How many of your past emotional pains have you identified and dealt with?

- Are there characteristics in your relationships today that remind you of your past?

- Do you control current relationships to battle repeating past hurts?

- How many of your failings to forgive and reconcile manifest desire in you to push someone else away or focus attention on them to draw them closer to you?

- Do you use people, places or things to make yourself feel better?

This book is written to help you recognize both failure and pain as God's way of allowing you to discover what you value most in all relationships, especially with Him. Pain shapes how we help others in faith, hope, and charity. Pain also requires us to forgive ourselves, and others, for past hurts. Forgiveness requires us to turn away from (repent) a self-centered hold on past hurts caused by any offense. In the aftermath of pain, we must stop from condemning and instead give of ourselves to rebuild and heal our own brokenness and that of our neighbors. We know we have forgiven completely when the act of giving produces a giddy joy in our hearts.

Way back in our fourth marriage counseling session, my wife and I disclosed to one another what we needed most from each other to help each other heal from past hurts we both felt. I pray God is using my healing with my wife to lead you to healing from past hurts, improving all your relationships, but especially yours with Him. The importance of a father's presence and validation is of paramount importance to us all. Without healing, decades of pain can build up in a man or woman and over time, they usually attempt to self-medicate their emotional pain with external stuff. Unresolved pain usually escalates into very destructive consequences to an individual when they self-medicate using people, places, or things to compensate for what they lack in emotional connectedness to others. Long-term emotional pain can stem from as far back to when children begin to interact on the playground at elementary school—embedding deep memory imprints of how the opposite sex thinks of you by how they treated you back then. The results can cause individuals to seek out compensating characteristics in future relationships for the rest of their lives—consciously or subconsciously.

The need to forgive is consistent to all human beings. Religion, movies, television, and actual life experiences demonstrate to us over and over the importance of forgiveness and reconciliation to our own emotional healing and future relationship success. Once you learn to recognize behavior patterns, you will no longer feel the need to judge, control or react. The patterns repeat so often that we sometimes cannot see the forest of need *we* have to forgive, reconcile, or just let go, through the wall of trees we have planted to hide our problems from the sight of others we strive to impress, connect and relate to.

An interesting example of this truth is played out in the incredibly successful Spider-Man© comic book made into a motion picture series. In the first movie the main character, Peter Parker, is being raised by his aunt and uncle when he is infected with super-spider-like powers by a laboratory test spider during a class trip. In the beginning, Peter attempts to use his new super-spider powers for his own personal gain and wins a wrestling match. The arena owner fails to pay Peter the prize money because Peter won the match in a much shorter time than what was stipulated in fine print. As Peter leaves the arena boss's office, feeling angry and entitled to the prize money, another man robs the arena boss at gunpoint and flees the scene right past Peter. Peter fails to stop the robber—even though, in that moment, he knows he should and could have—because of anger and a selfish view of the situation. Tragedy strikes Peter just moments later when the same robber Peter failed to stop murders his beloved uncle Ben who has been waiting outside for Peter.

Compounding Peter's guilt is his memory of his uncle Ben's advice that "with great power comes great responsibility." Peter grieves the loss of his uncle and turns away from using his powers selfishly to win money for himself. Peter makes a new covenant with himself to use his great strength and super-spider powers for the benefit of others, honoring his uncle Ben's advice. Throughout the rest of the *Spider-Man* movie series, each character that fails to forgive; pain and unresolved anger build up and *change* each character into a monster that offends the innocent people whom Spider-Man ends up having to defend. The effect of Peter's failure to forgive and protect the man at the arena when his uncle Ben was murdered ends up creating the Spider-Man we all know and love, who protects others from monsters with unresolved pain and anger that prey upon innocent people.

Anybody can become deluded by pain and resentment and choose to allow someone else to be hurt, too. Pain and resentment can and does infect us all. It is a universal problem.

You shall not bear hatred for your brother in your heart. Though you may have to reprove your fellow man, do not incur sin because of him. Take no revenge and cherish no grudge against your fellow countrymen. You shall love your neighbor as yourself. I am the Lord.

Leviticus 19 17:18

Do you want to move beyond emotional pain, resentment, anger, and *feel* the love you have starved for all your life?

This is an *important* undertaking and I promise it *will* happen over time. A human's sense of entitlement is another caustic character defect we sometimes succumb to. My therapist used the following analogy to explain entitlement to me: "A person wanted to buy a house, contacted a realtor, and established that they needed to save 20 percent of the purchase price. After a year, the buyer contacted the Realtor and stated they had indeed saved the down payment and were going to the casino to double their money. The person felt *entitled* to go to the casino because *they* had earned the money honestly and could choose to go if they wanted to. Entitlement blinds us to the negative consequences of our actions. The most obvious downside to gambling would be: loss of money, anger after the loss, and no house in the near future."

Past emotional hurts fester in our minds and hearts. Over time, unresolved pain causes us humans to "think" in ways that are like the preceding analogy. How many times have you or someone you know said, "It's my life, I can do what I want." Or, "If there is a God, he would not let this happen." Have you ever considered that human choices can sometimes subvert the good God has planned for us?

To follow are a few examples of God working in people's life to triumph over evil as His word in the Book of Exodus explains. The daughter of Pharaoh raised Moses privileged, and yet, as a young adult Moses was moved to rage and accidentally murders an Egyptian taskmaster, he witnessed mistreating a slave. Moses saves his own life by fleeing into the desert to escape Pharaoh's wrath. Moses' new life in the desert allows God to teach the Egyptian-raised Moses—the Nomad Shepherd (Hebrew) way of life. Moses is chosen by God to fulfill His covenant promise made to Abraham to bring Abraham's lineage into the Promise Land. Much more can be said of all the works of our tender, heavenly Father in Egypt, as the book of Exodus properly relates. In the end, Moses leads over six hundred thousand men, not counting women and children, plus flocks and herds of cattle and other livestock, out of Egypt. Moses delivers God's command to Pharaoh to let His people go. The book of Exodus teaches us the foundations of both the Jewish and Christian faiths. God's promise to Abraham was fulfilled 430 years after Joseph had resettled his father, brothers, and their wives and children during the years of famine that struck Egypt and the surrounding nations.

The famine that struck Egypt is found in the story of Joseph and is an incredible story of God using human weakness and jealousy to aid in relocating Israel to Egypt. Joseph continues to live a faithful life to God, after he was sold into slavery by his brothers. Joseph becomes Pharaoh's second in command over all of Egypt, decades after he was sold into slavery. (Please read Genesis, chapters 37 to 50.) Just think, 430 years after Joseph and his eleven brothers and their wives and children go into Egypt, Moses delivers their lineage out of Egypt as a tribal nation with over six hundred thousand men, plus their wives and children and livestock, into God's direct care and leadership; God leads them as a cloud by day and a pillar of fire by night. (Please read the book of Exodus, 13:21; Nehemiah 9:19.)

In the story of Joseph, it is related that Joseph has a different mother from ten of his siblings. It is also related that Joseph is most favored by his father. Are these emotions of jealousy, deceit, and anger used to crush Joseph altogether or serve God's holy will? As painful as Joseph's life in slavery and prison was to him, in the end, Joseph's life served God's will and was made part of His plan for the entire human race.

Both Bible stories teach that God is *always* at work in our lives. It is equally important to emphasize that both stories also teach that Moses and Joseph never became angry, bitter, or resentful towards God about the trials and circumstances of their lives, and thereby always had productive and meaningful relationship with others after they had sustained deep, emotional pain and hurt. Paramount to all their human relationships was their relationship and trust in God's will.

Whenever we need to wait on God (hopefully shorter than 430 years) or forgive someone, we need to turn to God's Word to help us understand how to survive our circumstance. Please read Isaiah 48:10-11.

The Book of Wisdom helps us understand what type of people Israel displaced, fulfilling God's transference of the Promise Land to Israel.

> For, truly, the ancient inhabitants of your holy land, whom you hated for deeds most odious- Works of witchcraft and impious sacrifices; a cannibal feast of human flesh and of blood, from the midst of... These merciless murderers of children, and parents who took with their own hands defenseless lives. You willed to destroy by the hands of our fathers, that the land that is dearest of all to you might receive a worthy colony of God's children. But even these, as they were men, you spared, and sent wasps as forerunners of your army that they might exterminate them by degrees. Not that you were without power to have the wicked vanquished in battle by the just, or wiped out at once by terrible beasts or by one decisive word. But condemning them bit by bit you gave them space for repentance. You were not unaware that their race was wicked and their malice ingrained, and that their dispositions would never change; for they were a race accursed from the beginning. Neither out of fear of anyone did you grant amnesty for their sins.
>
> The Book of Wisdom (12:3-11)

The Sanctity of Sex

The Lord spoke to Moses: "Speak to the Israelites and tell them, 'I, the Lord, am your God. You shall not do as they do in the land of Egypt, where you once lived, nor shall you do as they do in the land of Canaan, where I am bringing you; do not conform to there customs. My decrees you shall carry out, and my statutes you shall take care to follow. I, the Lord, am your God. Keep, then, my statutes and decrees, for the man who carries them out will find life through them. I am the Lord. None of you shall approach a close relative to have sexual intercourse with her. I am the Lord.

Leviticus Chapter 18 1:6

CHAPTER TWO

The Seven Swords of Sorrow

- How many times have you asked the question "Why, God?"

- How many times have you struggled to make sense of your own suffering, or the death of a child or another loved one?

- How many of your emotional wounds have not healed, regardless of how many different remedies you've tried?

- What do you use to soothe your emotional pain?

Often times, when we become acutely aware of someone's pain and circumstance, we wouldn't trade our problems with them for anything in this world. I once befriended a man named Larry who suffered through the separate and unrelated deaths of his mother, his uncle, and his brother; the loss of his house to a fire; and the loss of his wife through divorce—all in a short four-year span. You might mistakenly believe Larry had it coming, like the "friends" thought about Job, written about in the book of Job in the Bible. Larry's losses greatly increased my appreciation and thanksgiving to God for the protection of my entire family—before, during, and after my time away.

How much pain have you suffered in your life? Do you struggle to make sense of it? Do you resent God for things that have happened to you or your family?

How much better would you expect your life to be if you were chosen to be the mother of the Son of God Almighty? Would you mistakenly believe you'd be protected from pain and suffering automatically?

Have you ever contemplated how much pain and suffering Mary endured during her life as the mother of the Son of God? Do you know about the seven swords that pierced Mary's heart? Knowing more about what afflicted Mary's heart might help you to understand how God has chosen to help you to comprehend what you value most in your own life. What can we honestly expect *in* our lives when we comprehend some of the wounds that afflicted the Holy Family?

> For it is written; There are unseen powers at work that we must be armed against, and our Father in heaven is the only master-teacher of what truly works for our defense: selfless love (agape), empathy, and positive thinking—attracting good into our lives, and the lives of others. (Please read Colossians 1:16; Ephesians 6:12; 2 Corinthians 4:18).
>
> Mary's heart was pierced by the sword of sorrow seven times, all while establishing and caring for her family. The first sword of sorrow pierced Mary's heart upon hearing her Rabbi Simeon proclaim:
>
> And Simeon blessed them and said to Mary His mother; Behold this child is destined for the fall and rise of many in Israel, and to be a sign that will be contradicted and you yourself a sword will pierce so that the thoughts of many hearts will be revealed.
>
> Luke 2:34-35

How would you react to hearing your rabbi, or priest, proclaim about your child what Simeon did about Jesus to Mary? Would you dismiss the claims, be full of fear, or be at peace?

The second sword of sorrow pierced Mary's heart when Jesus's life was sought by King Herod. Angelic intervention was the causation for Joseph, Mary, and Jesus fleeing into Egypt under cover by the night, while King Herod's soldiers slaughtered boys two years of age and younger in the king's attempt to extinguish our Savior's life.

Six hundred years earlier, the prophet Jeremiah prophesied:

> A voice was heard in Ramah, sobbing and loud lamentation; Rachel weeping for her children and she would not be consoled, since they were no more.
>
> Matthew 2:18

Please read Matthew 2:13-18; Jeremiah 31:15.

Imagine the sorrow in your own heart, knowing that hundreds of children you knew of, or were your kin, were slaughtered by soldiers sent by a maniacal king looking to ensure your son did not disrupt his rule, as had been prophesied centuries earlier. How many children die in our current era because one parent, or both, strive to ensure their authority and lifestyles are not interrupted?

The third sword of sorrow pierced Mary's heart when Mary and Joseph realized they had unknowingly separated from Jesus after they traveled a day's journey, returning home from Passover when Jesus was twelve years old. After three days of searching, Jesus was discovered by his parents, while he was marveled at by the teachers in the temple as he revealed scripture to them, with Jesus responding to his parents concerns by saying:

> And he said to them, "Why were you looking for me? Did you not know that I must be in my father's house?"
>
> Luke 2:49

Please read Luke 2:41-52

How terrified would you feel if, after leaving a large party, you and your spouse discovered your twelve-year-old child was not within the group you traveled with, in this time of child abduction? And when you did find your child, after searching for three days, the child responded to you that you should have known he was in his father's house. How frightening would that be if you thought your child was brainwashed, or worse? How have you reacted to any child's special talent, or calling, when they yearned for independence?

The fourth sword of sorrow that pierced Mary's heart was when she went to meet Jesus on the Via-Delarosa, while Jesus carried his cross to Golgotha. Mary agonized, seeing Jesus's wounds after his scourging at the pillar and being brutalized with thousands of hits and kicks. He was bleeding all over his severely beaten body. While Mary desperately wanted to attend to Jesus, insults were being hurled at him from onlookers as he struggled to carry his burden on the way to the cross. Mary's attempts to get closer to him were thwarted by the crowd and garrison that drove him on to Golgotha. Simon, a Cyrenian, was pressed into service to pick up, and carry, Jesus's cross. Please read Luke 23:26.

Wouldn't every ounce of energy be drained out of you by the sight of your own son being brutalized beyond all description? Wouldn't you scream out, "Why, God?" from every inch of your being? Have you ever been forcibly separated from your child?

The fifth sword of sorrow pierced Mary's heart when she witnessed her son crucified for the sins of just and wicked souls alike. Mary stood by him at a distance, powerless to do anything to stop it from happening. Please read Luke 23:49; John 19:25.

Could you stand there and let your child die for the sins of other people? Could you die in the place of a strange criminal, as Jesus did for the good thief (Dismus) who was crucified next to him at Calvary?

Please read Luke 23:39-43.

The sixth sword of sorrow pierced Mary's heart when she watched Jesus die for three hours on the cross, all the while, watching Jesus pray and intercede for his enemies:

> Then Jesus said, "Father, forgive them, they know not what they do." They divided his garments by casting lots.
>
> Luke 23:34

Before commending his spirit into His Father's tender, caring hands, with his last breath."

Please read Luke 23:34-46.

Have you ever stayed by the side of your child, trying to comfort them as they died?

Can you imagine Mary's anguish?

The seventh sword of sorrow pierced Mary's heart when she saw his lifeless body enclosed in the tomb. Mary must have felt that Jesus' life was sought by those in authority, since the time he was born, all the while living a life of service to His Father in heaven and all who approached and requested His help and healing.

Please read John 19:28-42.

Have you ever buried a child of your own? Need I write anything more?

We can all dimly relate to one sorrow or another that Mary, Joseph, and Jesus persevered through, by having persevered through our own sufferings and life experiences. What we cannot fathom is Mary, Joseph, and Jesus having to carry the additional burden of watching their neighbors and loved ones suffer through it all as well over a thirty-three-year period.

What must you forgive of someone who has hurt you to be able to face Jesus, who died for you and your inability to be merciful to those in most need?

I believe that God, our tender and merciful Father, has continuously provided for all His creation and mourns our separation from Him, too. For it is written:

> Beloved, let us love one another, because love is of God; everyone who loves is begotten by God and knows God. Whoever is without love does not know God, for God is love. In this way the love of God was revealed to us: God sent his only Son into the world so that we might have life through him. In this is love: not that we have loved God, but that he loved us and sent his Son as expiation for our sins. Beloved, if God so loved us, we also must love one another. No one has ever seen God. Yet if we love one another, God remains in us, and his love is brought to perfection in us. This is how we know that we remain in him and he in us, that he has given us of his spirit.
>
> 1 John 4:7-13

> God knew from the beginning that only Jesus could endure rejection, abuse and injury, *and* fulfill the law: to love God the father completely and love others as God loves us.
>
> He came to what was his own, but his own people did not accept him.
>
> John 1:11

CHAPTER THREE

Root of Pain

The preceding chapters were written to firmly establish in your mind that we must expect pain in our lives. For a moment, consider your deepest fears and highest expectations that you had about your life since you were a child. My deepest sadness I felt as a child was watching people treat others with unkindness and brutality. I did not judge wrong doers but felt their loss, a kind of groaning by the Holy Spirit. A feeling that people were not going to make it to heaven. My mother convinced me that I could not "change the world" and I had to focus on my needs and those of others near to me in an attempt to calm me down and stop the downward spiral in my mental health she saw taking place at that time.

(Take time to write down *your* answers to questions posed throughout this book so that you can review your feelings about forgiveness and your relationship with our heavenly Father and everyone else in your life.)

What was your life supposed to be like? Was it supposed to be a comfortably numb feeling, between depression and jubilation? If you are like most people, there are huge departures from what you hoped to become in youth, from what you feel you are now. Does joy occupy your heart or does emotional agony or resentment occupy your mind?

Was there abuse in your family? Do you dread family functions over the holidays? Or do you look forward to coming together as a family?

How does your relationship with God fit into your pursuit of happiness and freedom from your past? What do you think God has withheld from you? How do you feel abandoned by God? How has God let you down? Be honest; write down all your responses. It's easier to write the page number and your response to the questions in their order.

Do you think you really know your heavenly Father?

Without looking, what page of the 1,400-plus pages of the Holy Bible do you think details the account of the flood wherein God washes the face of the earth clean of all His creation, to start fresh through a *new* covenant with Noah? If you are like most people, you can't say with certainty where the story is told in the Holy Bible. Most people guess, saying, halfway through the Bible. Surprisingly, the flood is detailed in chapters six through nine of Genesis. Chapter six of Genesis is normally found on or around the *sixth page* of most Holy Bibles. The flood relates God's one and only "do-over." At the end of chapter nine, God promises to never wipe out all of creation again. God marks the skies with rainbows for all time, to remind Himself and all earth's inhabitants of His covenant to Noah, through whom our lineage flows. Please read God's promise in Genesis 9:8-17.

You may be wondering—what is the importance of God's covenants to you? It's important for you to realize that, like most people, through ignorance, you may be living separated from God like the people did in the days of Noah—abandoning our heavenly Father through the choices you make, in a life outside of what Jesus teaches, for an increase of your own happiness. The Holy Bible is really *His story* about His love for His children and the lengths He goes to throughout history to restore *His* relationship with His children in this life and for eternity in the next. God makes His covenants known so that souls can choose to come home to Him by asking for His forgiveness, like St. Dismus did, hanging on the cross next to Jesus, before death overtook him. Please read the forgiveness of Dismus found in Luke 23:39-43.

If one persists to abandon God, our Father reluctantly and woefully accommodates stubborn souls in their desire to be separated from Him in a place where He is not—like God has done for Lucifer. The abyss is referred to in Psalm 16:10; Romans 10:5-13; Revelations 17:8; Acts 2:27.

Did you know you were *stolen* from your Heavenly Father? How would knowledge of *you* being stolen from your heavenly Father, with you being infected with a *permanent emotional imbalance*, affect how you feel about your relationship with God now? Could you then see our tender Father's true intentions and lengths He would go to restore your relationship with Him?

Are you intrigued to know more about God's plan for what makes your soul the happiest? Read God's plan, revealed in Isaiah 48:17- 22.

His story of how we were stolen from Him begins with God having open relationship with Adam and Eve in the Garden of Eden, written in the book of Genesis. Genesis 3 tells us about our Root-Pain. Resentment and malice is *our* root pain, and that of our children's children, if the correction program taught through the life of Christ Jesus is not accepted and uploaded into the core of our being. Jesus our Rabbi, which means teacher, shows us His Father; who is love, unity, trust, reconciliation and forgiveness; for us all. God wants to remove the deception that began in the garden of Eden. Please read Genesis 3 then 2 Corinthians 11:3.

You literally have an eternity in either instance, so indulge me a little.

Before Adam and Eve were made, Lucifer was a highly favored angel doing God's business in the heavens and on earth. Lucifer, like some humans, felt like he was doing all the work—and the boss (God) was getting all the glory and having an easier time of it. Lucifer decided he could do it all for himself. In essence, spinning off from God, and going into business separately. Lucifer announced to his fellow angels that any one of them that wanted to continue to work for him could, and in that, they needed to follow him. God honored Lucifer's desires to be separated from Him and cast Lucifer and the other angels who wanted to follow Lucifer from His presence. In the final judgment, all of God's creation that chooses to be separated from Him will be defeated by the Lamb of God and separated from His chosen; cast into the lake of fire ever burning and yet never consumed for eternity. Read Revelation 17:8-14.

God then created Adam and Eve to be His new caretakers of the earth (Genesis 2:7). Lucifer's replacements were made from the dust of the earth (Ecclesiastes 3:20), which added insult to injury, infuriating Lucifer beyond description. Seething with bitterness and resentment; vengeance became Lucifer's preferred spiritual diet. Lucifer opened the eyes of both Adam and Eve to the knowledge of both good and evil in the garden of Eden. God is pure Love and goodness. *Introducing the knowledge of good and evil into Adam and Eve stole them from God,* **and** *it was cold, calculated vengeance.* (if not already read...Please read Genesis 3:1-7)

The story of Adam and Eve is literally the root of our pain. Our thoughts, feelings, and actions emulate those of Lucifer's (evil) when we feel *justified* in hostility towards others; feeling entitled to cause others pain. We sometimes act-out like Lucifer when we feel victimized or have suffered pain. In contrast, we are instructed to Love as the fulfillment of the Law. Read Romans 13:8-10.

Anti-Christ like behavior is feeling entitled to hurt someone because they hurt us first. Christ like behavior is to empathize that they too are hurting and to forgive and reconcile with them, as God our Father strives to do with us, through Christ Jesus. God knows we suffer as a result of our fall in the garden. God also knows we suffer because of our knowledge of both Good and Evil. We sometimes mistakenly feel entitled and justify our actions—like Lucifer did—in vengeance, when we feel we've been deceived, taken advantage of, or victimized.

Our pain becomes our sole focus, distorting our thoughts, feelings, and actions, and numbing us to the needs of others (Psalm 56). The corruption of persecuting others has resided in our cognitive process ever since Adam and Eve considered what Lucifer presented about their needs being paramount to their relationship with God—their creator. Pain, resentment and retaliation is our permanent emotional imbalance. Lucifer used what he was angry about to put fear in Adam and Eve, and all their descendants. Instilling in all humans the fear that God had failed to tell *us* the whole truth about death and all of God's creation. (if not already; see Genesis 3:4-5)

Have *you* ever really given God a chance to lead you to your happiness? Jesus was born to teach us all what God wants us to know. Jesus is the Word incarnate (John 1:14), freeing us of the bondage of sin, brokenness and self-doubt; Jesus born to make our souls His temple residence (1 Corinthians 3:17). Jesus continues to teach us through the power of His Holy Spirit and The Word of God to properly focus on ministering to the needs of others and ourselves in "fulfillment of the law" *versus* earning our way into Heaven through offerings and rituals.

In my Bethesda Family Services parenting class, we studied a relationship cycle that taught us that when trust and mutuality are broken, one becomes offended. It also teaches that if we do not reconcile with one another immediately after trust is broken, our emotional error is to selfishly dwell on our pain, causing us to become bitter and resentful over time. Our pain then distorts our thinking to the point that we can justify choosing to act in hostility toward others in ways that cause them to experience our pain—just like Lucifer's actions separating us from God our Father. My wife and I recently discovered that, through her father's failings, she projected how she felt about her father, then, onto all my verbal interactions with her in the recent past.

Television, familial relations, and even animal behavior plays this offense cycle out before us, in plain sight, constantly, every day, in everything that exists on our planet.

Quick examples are:

- A monkey steals a banana from another. The second retaliates and attacks the first. As a result of the first offense, any other monkey that comes close to the first monkey's bananas will be attacked.

- Someone cuts you off while driving. So you feel justified in tailgating them, or worse. Each additional similar instance increases your sense that the roads are *full* of insensitive people and you start to act-out your irritation.

- You don't have enough money. So you feel justified in paying your creditor late, if at all. You may even borrow more, just to make ends meet, increasing the feeling that your life is out of control.

- A spouse forgets an important anniversary. So the one wounded withholds affections. After withholding affections, an increased feeling of abandonment occurs if the disconnect is not identified and talked about.

- Deception is identified. So, you never trust them again and make their life miserable. After a period of time you feel guilty over your persecution, and try to make up with the deceiver.

Taking those examples above, what if:

- The monkey that stole was given another banana by the first, teaching him how to share his food with others through example?

- The person cut off by the driver gave the other space and received peace from it?

- You call your creditor, acknowledge the delay, and plan a different payment cycle date?

- The hurt spouse shows concern for the other spouse and asks what's going on in their life that would displace the memory of the most important day of their lives?

- The one deceived asks point-blank, what have I done to you to cause you to lie to me?

Part of the infinite wisdom imparted to us through Christ Jesus teaches us never to return evil for evil. Strive for unity and connection. Turn the other cheek. These are simple examples of how we can choose to never offend again, especially when we *think* our retaliation is justified.

Lucifer has attempted to usurp our relations with the kingdom of heaven by attacking our imperfection; always.

> Then I heard a loud voice in heaven saying, "Now have salvation and power come, and the kingdom of our God and the authority of his anointed. For the accuser of our brothers is cast out, who accuses them before our God day and night.
>
> Revelation 12:10.

Our greatest personal challenge is to distance ourselves from the debilitating mindset of feeling justified in our acting out...but instead always striving for unity; having compassion for another's shortcomings; forgiving them without getting even, operating solely in the frame work God intended us to operate in, from *our* beginning in the garden of Eden; and depending and living on a constant diet of faith, hope, and dependency on God the Father who is love and charity.

> Deceit is in the hands of those who plot evil, but those who counsel peace have joy.
>
> Proverbs 12:20

God's story enlightens us to how distorted our thinking can become.

Have you rejected God and accepted Lucifer's testimony in the Garden—that our heavenly Father withheld the whole truth from us?

Do you believe Satan's lie—that God only told us we'd die because He didn't want us to be His equals?

Knowledge of good and evil enables us to feel *entitled* to act out our indignation and justify hurting others back. I believe God wanted to protect us all from acting out our pain and resentment towards one another. Our heavenly Father's deepest desire is for all His children to forgive and forget the hurts and pain that cause us to angrily justify hurting others back. Jesus taught us in the Lord's Prayer that we ask our Father to *forgive our sins, as we forgive those who sin against us.* The key is: forgiveness is only given to those who forgive—mercy for the merciful. Our release of blame creates capacity in our mind, heart, and soul for God's Spirit to reside in us, consoling us, while teaching faith, hope and love. God's Holy Spirit protects us from our self-centered righteousness.

Anger and Vengeance: Grave News
Monday April 16, 2007

If you think pain, bitterness, and retaliation require long periods to fester—tell that to the families of the thirty-three dead and twenty wounded young adults of Virginia Tech's massacre today.

Tender, merciful Father in heaven, please let the souls of all these poor victims, and their families, rest with you when you call them—even the depraved soul who in a fit of rage over a break up with his girlfriend committed this devastating, destructive act of anger and vengeance.

God's wisdom teaches us to stand guard at all times against the ensnaring mindset of resentment. Anger is like a thief in the night that steals the precious souls you love, guard, and protect. Unresolved anger in another can be the catalyst to massive devastation, destruction, and consequence.

To love and when rejected; learn to forgive, make new agreements, let go and move beyond.

CHAPTER FOUR

Miss-Matched Expectations

Think again about the questions posed in the beginning of chapter one:

- How much of your past emotional pains have you identified and dealt with?

- Are there characteristics in your relationships today that remind you of your past?

- Do you control current relationships to battle repeating past hurts?

- How many of your failings to forgive and reconcile manifest desire in you to push someone else away or focus attention on them to draw them closer to you?

- Do you use people, places or things to make yourself feel better?

ow ponder: When choosing your mate—did you consciously delve into past successes and failures in relationships with others, to understand what you both value most in a potential relationship *together*?

Today's divorce rate reflects the fear we have in openly sharing our past hurts with others. Studies report that almost half of this year's marriages will end in divorce. Couples do not know how to trust and openly express their vulnerabilities, creating more miss-matched expectations and offense with their new partners.

Do you keep up appearances? Do you feel vulnerable to loss holding in fears and hurts?

Rather than expressing the hurts caused to our hearts, or those we have caused to past loved ones, we press onward, formulating new relationship risk-versus-reward appraisals based on physical attributes, competencies, scholastic achievement, and bank account balances. The more we *stuff* past pain, the more we tend to medicate it with other diversions such as materialism, emotional and chemical dependencies, and sexual addictions. Most people try to change how they feel on the inside by using and controlling "external stuff." You might have attempted to control how you feel by holding back, cancelling plans and distancing yourself. Trying to change how you feel might become more complicated. For example, moving out of your residence and starting the formal separation process from your mate. However, *no matter where you go, there you are*. After the changes are made, the root feelings you attempted to relieve will still be part of you, and your relationship may continue with greater complexity.

A husband and wife should be equally yoked—this statement is enriched by understanding that when *oxen* are equally yoked they pull together side-by-side, effectively tilling mass areas of land. Wooden yokes over oxen heads, along with the harnesses, distribute the burden between the two oxen equally. Like humans, oxen are creatures of habit and sometimes pull their burden in slightly opposing directions, causing damage to one or both necks over time. The heavier the burden (more stress), the easier it is for their wounds to become exasperated with disease, and death is an outcome if their handler does not intervene and correct their miss-matched directional pull.

What this analogy conveys is that when our relationship with others is heavily burdened by stressors, any imbalance of soul (thoughts, feelings and actions) can cause one or both parties in the relationship to pull in different directions. Death to the relationship occurs over time if the emotional pain that causes stress to one or both parties is not disclosed, forgiven and new agreements made to stop the creation of stress from happening again. Without disclosure, husband and wife experience increasing discomfort in their relationship because of their emotional hurt, their sense that the other is indifferent to their needs, and that the other fails to turn toward the direction their own life experience dictates them to choose. This increases fear in both, and each one's perception that the *other* mate just doesn't understand what's important to them. Trauma and offense occur when husband or wife pull harder and harder in the direction each is more inclined to pull toward, while yoked by their bond of marriage.

My wife felt emotionally disconnected from her father. She grew up feeling like he did not value her. He was addicted to television and paid very little attention to her. When he did take the time to acknowledge her, he acted put off by it. The consequences of these early memory imprints was that my wife saw our marital interactions with a mind filter that was on the defense against these same types of hurts from me.

Bethesda Family Services Foundation taught me in their parenting class that a healthy soul is clear of unresolved anger and inner conflict, and has a balance of the three expressions of the inner soul: intellect, emotions, and will.

Bethesda defines soul as the balance of:

- Intellect: your cognitive process—how you think. How you think is strongly influenced by memories and life experiences with your thoughts acting like triggers for your emotions. We learned that by changing your thinking you are able to change how you feel.

- Emotions: which include your attitudes and the range of feelings you experience about your thoughts and ideas, and past, present, or future expectations.

- Will: your motivations, decisions, actions, and behaviors.

Bethesda's parenting class taught us that in healthy relationships the three expressions of soul (thoughts, feelings, and actions) are in balance when one does not overpower the other. If one partner in the relationship has unresolved pain, grief, or anger from a past wound, the balance of soul (thoughts, feelings and actions) becomes disrupted. We think, and then we have feelings about those thoughts, and in turn we act out those feelings and thoughts in behavior. Any imbalance of soul is amplified when the pain is hidden and the person seeks out ways to medicate their pain (i.e. alternative relationships, sex, alcohol, drugs, pain relievers, lust, power, or control).

Fear and bitterness may cause your emotions to override your intellect, impacting your actions with impulsive self-destructive and regrettable behavior. An example: fear of abandonment may cause you to telephone your partner to check where they are and when they are coming back more often than if you did not have the underlying fear.

Have you ever felt like your past keeps repeating? How have you used sex to medicate your emotional pain?

Bethesda taught when people experience broken trust in a relationship, the natural tendency is to immediately retaliate by pushing the other away, or to withdraw and detach emotionally by becoming quiet, leaving the room, or canceling a planned event.

How many times have you turned to a third party to complain about your loved one? Talking with a third party may help you, but your mate does not have a chance to keep up. When you disclose your hurts to a third party, the one you need to reconcile with is never given the opportunity to fully understand your needs. This creates more misunderstandings between the two mates in the future.

In the past, how have you and your mate responded to disappointments? Do you fight for what you want? Or do you strive to understand the experiences your mate has had that form the foundation of their unique perspective? How do you continue the goodness you both felt in the beginning of your relationship after the honeymoon is over?

Do you feel it is unfair that your mate desires unconditional love—continuing your marriage beyond what you feel is a reconcilable difference? Till death do we part? Are you stubborn? Is your heart hardened? (Please read Mathew 19:6-8.)

Everybody's experience in life is different. Some people criticize our parents' generation for staying together for their children's sake. My wife's parents modeled staying together for the sake of their children during her upbringing. Did your parents model unconditional love while you were being raised? Did one of your parents favor one child over the other(s)? How is that child doing emotionally, now that they are trying to win the affections of their current partners? How does performance and reward affect their happiness?

The soul of a family is the culmination of thoughts, emotions, and actions witnessed from childhood till now, defining what we are most comfortable with in relationship with others. How would that change your view of your relationships knowing more about the family history of ideas, emotions, and actions in those most important to you? Culture is important, and diversity can be very conflicted. God's history taught through the Holy Bible can be a productive means to achieve consistency between all families. Please read Deuteronomy 32:1-16.

Before my wife, I had wanted to marry for a long time, but had suffered through a lot of loneliness and bad choices with women before I was introduced to her. After being introduced to my wife, I purposely chose her, early on in our relationship, to be my wife. I did this for many reasons, but most of all because my wife and I had talked about why we both had left prior relationships. She and I had grown up several towns apart and her life was very focused on family which was very important to me.

My wife and I had both struggled over a long period of time trying to find the right mate. We had both given our trust over to God to supply a mate, and had waited on God for a couple of years to bring His choice of *that* mate into our lives. I loved my wife's Greek heritage and customs. I loved how easy it was to just spend time with my wife. She was at ease with all the activities we chose to do on the weekends. She wasn't demanding and needy for attention. She had a career. And most importantly—to me, we seemed to have similar aspirations for family and work. We were ready for God's answer to our prayers for Him to supply each of us our life mates, and yet, it took five years of courtship before my wife and I married.

My wife and I were introduced to each other by the members of my prayer group when we attended a steeplechase in New Jersey in 1994. That first evening in October we had gone back to the farmhouse where I was living and enjoyed port wine on the screened porch where I wooed her, reading excerpts from a novel titled *Care of the Soul* by Thomas Moore.

My wife had always wanted her mate to read romantically to her—something I had no prior knowledge about. That night, while reading to her, I asked my wife if I could kiss her, which met the standards she sought in her mate for civility and charisma. I was just being myself, and in that I was totally unaware of how much this meant to my wife until years later. I found significance in that evening too, but in an entirely different way. *Care of the Soul* uses Mr. Moore's practice in psychiatry, coupled to Greek mythology and Bible scripture, to delve into how we organize our lives, and how the universe acts in direct response to the yearnings of our souls. From the moment my wife and I had met, it was clear to me that there were actions we had both taken, way before our introduction, which had brought us together. I wanted a life mate I could take care of and be very romantic with. My wife wanted an old-fashioned romance, too. *Care of the Soul* taught us that relationships are an outcome of conscious and unconscious yearnings of the soul—we have asked for and received what we yearn for, good or bad. *Care of the*

Soul is an extremely deep read. Another powerful book is, *The Secret* in which one of its teachings is how to draw the best into our lives from the power of *gratitude*.

Bethesda's Family Service Foundation's parenting classes taught me that a soul without love is often overtaken by fear, bringing torment into the life of that person. This fear infects the person's emotions and spirit. Fear and love cannot exist in the same heart. People who experience feelings of fear are at risk for increased levels of rage, personal vengeance, bitterness, depression, drug and alcohol problems, interpersonal conflict, and addictions of every type. As long as fear exists in the soul and is not cast out, the individual will continue to experience a sense of distress and defeat. Please read 2 Timothy 1:7.

Until my time away from my wife in treatment, I did not know how to identify with what my wife was feeling or why. After we were married in 1999, my wife's fear focused on our financial future and grew to the point that it caused her to shut down emotionally. Like a physical wound, soul imbalances make us hypersensitive when people touch on related subjects, with the hurt causing us to withdraw and disconnect further. As my wife's fear loomed larger we failed to trust and openly communicate how we were feeling. I mistakenly perceived her fear as doubt in my abilities, and became very defensive. As our mismatched perceptions played out over time, we both felt like the other just did not understand what was important, and normal marital relations died. I tried desperately to compensate her doubts by doing nearly everything around the house and taking trips around the entire country looking into new business partnerships.

Our son was born in February 2001 and until our daughter's conception in October 2002, I was unable to connect with my wife because my own fear had grown to the point that I obsessed over the smallest details of our lives together. I failed to balance my fear with the need to provide for any of the stability my wife needed.

In Bethesda's parenting class I learned that Deilia is a level of fear that paralyzes those who have it from trusting others (Deilia— from the Greek *deos*, meaning "dread"). Deilia causes those who are afflicted by it to shut down emotionally, trapping them in a cycle of distress, with fear short-circuiting every relationship. We were taught that each person's ability to freely and intimately connect with others is critical to one's sense of healthy fulfilling relationship. If you are comfortable sharing your thoughts and aspirations with those closest to you, but conceal your most painful memories and fears, your intimacy will be greatly hindered. The trauma from remembering your most painful memories may hinder you sharing them, ever. There might be fear of further rejection which restricts your freedom from sharing more deeply.

My fear had grown to cause me to react to my wife in ways that caused her to stop trying to help me understand her better. How many men do you know who are capable of sharing their fears? All men must be encouraged to open up, to move beyond their fear, and to trust and give up controlling outcomes. My career success was greatly diminished by my inability to communicate well with my wife. Feeling disconnected from my wife impacted how well I connected with clients and impacted my career success, which feed directly back into my wife's concerns.

> For this very reason, make every effort to supplement your faith with virtue, virtue with knowledge; knowledge with self-control; self-control with endurance, endurance with devotion; devotion with mutual affection; mutual affection with love. If these are yours and increase in abundance, they will keep you from being idle or unfruitful in the knowledge of our Lord Jesus Christ.
>
> 2 Peter 1:5-8

Pope John Paul II wrote and preached: Do Not Fear.

He is like someone calculating the cost in his mind. "Eat and drink," he says to you, but his heart is not with you.

Proverbs 23:7

God's love grows our trust and diminishes our fear. How much control has been authorized by citizens to governments because fear continues to consume all minds and hearts, especially these last fifteen years?

Bethesda's parenting classes taught me that the best way to draw closer to those you love is to risk sharing the truth about your emotional pain from your past that causes "extremes" in your own thoughts, feelings, and actions. I have learned that the way to overcome my own fear is to talk about what makes me afraid openly. Without this depth of honesty, the trust level in any relationship is weakened, and you cannot experience the immense trust from being completely honest and vulnerable with those that love *you*. Emotional intimacy involves sharing your feelings when you are hurt, happy, sad, fearful, confident, etc. It's a willingness to become vulnerable by opening your heart. It involves a genuine feeling of safety, security, and acceptance between you and another person; in spite of your fear of unknown outcomes from sharing sensitive information.

Before my treatment, instead of turning to my wife and opening up about my fears, I shared them with someone else instead. How often have you turned to confide in a friend, and not the one you should? The results are always the same: we grow closer to the one we place our confidence in and further away from the one we should be honest with and open up to.

In Bethesda's parenting classes, we also learned that every man, woman, and child has an overwhelming hunger for this depth of connection and intimacy. It is connection we starve for and seek to satisfy beyond any conflict our relationships can experience. We always strive for connection, even when the circumstances of our life attack the integrity of our bond with another. We must learn to disclose our fears, and listen to concerns others have, forgive, make new agreements, let go and move beyond offense.

My wife has truly waited for me to learn what I desperately needed to learn, so that I could come back to her, free of my pain, and fulfill my vows.

If every man, woman, and child hungers for connection and intimacy, then is it possible for you to see our tender Father in heaven from whom we are made in the image of, as being driven beyond our separation to completely reconcile with *you,* His child? The Bible is God's word and extends deep connection about the past pain God has suffered as a result of the fall of Adam and Eve in the Garden of Eden. God conveys these deep hurts in an effort to establish deep intimacy with us. He uses past pains to establish what is most important for our relationship *with Him.* Can you see others in your life striving to forgive you and reconcile with you, too? Who have *you* turned away from, and, who have you turned to when you were hurt? God's history of reconciliation is manifested through His new covenant with His children, time and again, and is our pattern for reconciliation with Him and everyone else in our lives. God continues to extend agreements to us through His representatives, enabling His love and providence over us, beyond our separation from Him in the garden of Eden. God always chooses unity and a genuine selfless affection that endures beyond the greatest conflict His relationship with us can ever experience. Please read; Ezekiel 45:17; Malachi 3:6; Hebrews 9:12; 2 Corinthians 5:18.

To love and when rejected; learn to forgive, make new agreements, let go and move beyond.

We are made in the image of our Father. We starve to be known, understood, appreciated, respected and included. God wants *us* to know Him, understand Him, appreciate Him, respect Him and include Him. He does not ask for all our time, and knows we cannot fully comprehend Him but desires our respect and appreciation and wants us to include Him in our lives. True happiness comes from knowing, understanding, appreciating, respecting and including all our loved ones...especially God.

In contrast; the enemy wants us to feel like no-one knows us, no-one understands us, no-one appreciates us, no-one respects us and no-one includes us. When we feel utterly alone, abandoned and UN-loved and then someone mistakenly hurts us -we go to war. We feel totally justified and act out; which is exactly what the enemy of our Heavenly Father wants us to do. Judging, sentencing and putting to death another soul for whom we should recognize is hurting just like we are and we should in the Spirit of Truth; Forgive, Reconcile with and Let Go.

Jesus teaches when we judge another, we then are judged similarly by His Father in heaven. Our actions are like a boomerang and come back to us in the form of how we put them out there towards another soul. Luke 6: 35-38

CHAPTER FIVE

Love Distorted by Fear and Pain

Try to remember and write down the names of all those you have loved and then abandoned because you were resentful or brokenhearted, or just plain selfish.

Has fear ever driven you to act against your better judgment?

Have you ever reached out and tried to connect with someone, even though you knew there might be really bad consequences as a result of it?

Bethesda Family Services Foundation parenting classes taught me that a soul without love is often overtaken by fear, bringing torment into the life of that person. This fear infects the person's emotions and spirit. Fear and love cannot exist in the same heart. People who experience feelings of fear are at risk for increased levels of rage, personal vengeance, bitterness, depression, drug and alcohol problems, interpersonal conflict, and addiction of every type. As long as fear exists in the soul and is not cast out, the individual will continue to experience a sense of distress and defeat.

My time away in therapy enabled me to identify a pattern of behavior in me that I had not before. I abandon people when I am emotionally wounded by them. In my teens I had learned to use alcohol and sex to salve my emotional wounds. And when I was really hurt, I'd nuke the relationship by abandoning the person, and then use alcohol and sex with another person to numb my pain. I hid my emotional pain and didn't disclose it honestly with the women I cared about, to heal our relationship and move beyond the hurt and offense I suffered from.

My pattern of abandonment started when I was about six years old. My neighbor, Mike and I were friends and played together well, and often. One day, Mike had another friend named Greg over. Greg was from our neighborhood, but lived much farther away from Mike than I did. Mike and Greg were saying hurtful things to me and I angrily asked them to stop, and when they didn't, I threatened not to be their friend anymore. They laughed, and I walked away, and when they called out saying they were only kidding, I only glanced back once. When we'd see one another in the hallway at school, we were cordial, but we failed to restore our friendship to what it might have been if that morning's exchange never occurred.

From that point in my life, the pattern replicated itself with others. When I was twenty-three, Suzanne left me for Patrick, and I drank, nearly killing myself behind the wheel of a V8 Mustang. When Maureen cheated on me, I never spoke to her again, and then hooked up with her friend. Barbra and I had a love that lasted eight years. When we separated my heart ached, but I never went back to rekindle our relationship.

During my time away, I learned, through introspection, about my destructive pattern, and why people might choose to become hermits, too. It's self-preservation. I'm too dependent on approval by others of me and I become self-destructive after the loss of a relationship when it occurs. I guess that's why I've always done well with sales, because I genuinely try to earn my client's respect and their business to a fault.

My wife and I wrote our vows for one another a year before we married, during our betrothal. Our vows were an expression borne out of what we desired most from one another. My vow to my wife was that I would not let her raise our children alone. My wife's vow to me was that she would not lose respect for me. When I asked my wife to make her vow to me, I explained to my wife that for most of my life people seemed to become complacent in relationship with me and then take me for granted.

My work as a sales person over the past four decades requires me to meet or exceed past performance objectives. I was conditioned to perform, then receive my reward—a commission bonus. My work helped me achieve a level of emotional connectedness with others through our sharing of business ideas, our feelings about family life, and our motivations for doing business together. Part of my marital problems stemmed from my conditioning at work, wherein I expected recognition after I performed. Relationships don't function like jobs; they are far more complex.

By early 2002 I had a tremendous need for attention that was not being met. I went from working in a fast-paced New Jersey-based company in June 2000 to starting my new job—working from a home-based office, which took me six months to adjust to. Finally, I adjusted to the change in early 2001, and then Anthrax engulfed my industry with fear and unknown variables. September 11th 2001 made things far worse.

When my wife and I began to have marital problems in mid-2001, I mistakenly tried to earn her love and respect by doing good all the time—compulsively cleaning our home, taking care of our children, making meals, and working. I grew more and more intense, as I hoped that, if I made my wife happy by taking care of everything, she'd see how important our relationship was to me, and our relations would normalize. I now know that I contributed to my wife shutting down and withdrawing from me by sending signals of distress and fear, which impacted her. She felt abandoned by me, emotionally, and judged by me. I generally keep schedules and plan things in advance, but in my fear, I took things to a fervent level, consequently, making my wife feel like I didn't trust her abilities. My overcompensation caused my wife to withdraw further, causing me to try to compensate more. I wasn't being honest with her about my fears and I communicated what I could in a way that was confounding to her, driving her further away from me. We both had tunnel vision caused by our fears. Now I know that by taking over everything I was making my wife feel like I had no trust in her abilities whatsoever.

My wife and I had taken on so many life-stressors in a very short period after our wonderful courtship of five years. We hosted a beautiful, traditional wedding and reception, and then enjoyed a happy honeymoon. We then purchased our dream home in a nearby state and moved. I began my new job working from home. My son was born, happy and healthy, eight months after our move. Twenty-three months after our wedding, Anthrax in the USPS mail system caused massive changes in the printing and mailing industry in which I worked. People adopted Internet marketing out of necessity. Printing and mailing was further impacted by postage increases and paper resource conservation for planet conservation.

Both my wife and I were experiencing normal first marriage growing pains from all the changes we had taken on in our lives together, compounded by the changes we had no control over. On top of all the fear that my wife and I were experiencing in our lives, there was the unresolved pain and resentment I felt about other relationships.

Before proceeding, I want to repeat the questions posed at the beginning of the chapter for emphasis.

- Try to remember and write down the names of all those you have loved and then abandoned, because you were angry and brokenhearted, or just plain selfish.

- Has fear ever driven you to act against your better judgment?

- Have you ever reached out and tried to connect with someone, even though you knew there might be really bad consequences as a result of it?

With Bethesda Family Services' help, I'd learned that every soul has an insatiable hunger to feel completed by the love from another individual whom they love. Every human being enters this world reaching out for this love, just as the hands of the infant reach out for the affectionate embrace of their mother. Bethesda teaches there is no fear in love, but love casts out fear because fear brings torment. Only real love is capable of fulfilling the human heart. True intimacy is love that connects on—thoughts, feelings, and actions together with the one you love. Torment of every kind will manifest in the heart and life of humans who have unresolved pain and fear, such as depression, despondency, suicidal ideation, panic, personality disorders, interpersonal conflict, and much more. Torment leads to one's desperate search for counterfeit substitutes that take them deeper into bondage: drugs, alcohol, lust, power, control, etc. Fear must be identified, confronted, and cast out. This battle is to be active, not passive, and requires the total investment of the one in bondage. When fear is cast out, the healing can begin.

Neither my wife or I felt any satisfaction by being known by the other, understood by the other, appreciated by the other, respected by the other or included by the other. We were devoid of affection and trust for one another. We were dead to one another.

CHAPTER SIX

What to Expect When You Go to Prison

f rejection, fear, and anger are the primary causes of offending, how can prisoners come out healed and ready to function better if they haven't learned how to deal with pain, resentment, fear, rejection, and abandonment—using healthy, coping skills?

Although my time in prison was not devoid of personal growth and introspection, it still causes me to feel great distress, remembering the pain I caused my family; trying to make sense of how I could depart from the person they knew and loved for so long—to the person I became with such a great need to get pain, anger, and bitterness out of my soul (thoughts, feelings, and behaviors).

Having said that, this chapter will not be about the fairness I think may or may not exist in our judicial system. It is not about how to circumvent the pitfalls society places in the paths of those men, women, and children who act out in conflict, with laws God and our society preserve. I *will* provide you a glimpse of my experiences before and during confinement.

Disclosing details of my secret pain in therapy for the first time was like releasing the contents of a soda bottle after having shaken it. I discharged the contents of my guilt and pain, which had contorted my thoughts, feelings, and actions for such a longtime. I tearfully related everything that had happened and the sergeant began crying with me, too. After I was through telling her everything, she asked her superior to come into the office and for me to explain it all to him as well. At the end of the second telling of my story, he attempted to console me by saying that he did not hold ill will toward me, and that he had had experiences investigating other circumstances to which my situation paled in comparison. They then explained to me that the district attorney would make a determination as to whether or not I would be *charged* by the state for my behavior. It wasn't about me making financial restitution to an individual. The venue quickly turned to how I would compensate the *public.*

It was another couple of hours that I sat handcuffed to a rail in the police station. I was never read my Miranda rights, as was evidenced in later courtroom testimony by the sergeant. I was then led to the municipal magistrate's court to be appraised of my charges.

Be forewarned that courtroom proceedings usually have a gallery of reporters hawking that day's events to feed a readership ready to consume reports about vulgar debtors. The magistrate informed me of the charges that related to the claim made by the affiant police sergeant and set bail, advising me that I was very fortunate and that she would remand me to stay local, to avail myself to all the processes that she set forth, including weekly reporting requirements to the local pre-trial services department. The magistrate advised me that I was to act on everything pre-trial services requested, as if the request itself had come from her, which I did. From that point, my life was not my own and was filled by interview after interview with psychologists, administrators, and therapists.

If you are one whose character is open and not littered with hatred and hostility, most people you come in contact with during these measurement processes are seasoned to recognize your vulnerability. Each attempted to console me about the journey they knew was going to take place.

Since I plead guilty, there was no trial. I could not put my innocent family, or our community through the horrific and traumatizing experience a trial would subject them to. Subsequent articles did inflict additional injury to my family and community whenever my debtor was referenced in court proceedings.

Friends and neighbors declared to me, privately, that they had been consumed by shock for days from the published allegations. Some said they required several days off from work to recover from the pain and betrayal they felt. A few neighbors and long time friends have supported me through the entire process, knowing that my story will help create differentiation, awareness and healing.

One county probation officer put it best—if it was just a few years earlier, I would have probably received county probation as a sentence. But, these times required a more sobering sentencing scheme. After all, my sentencing judge had been featured for almost eight months prior to my sentencing on a nightly national news syndicate as "soft."

During my sentencing, I received a standard range sentence. Not mitigated, nor aggravated. I was devastated because I felt that my cooperation in the testing, as well as my contrition, would have helped the court view me as remorseful. My wife and sister sat sobbing just a couple of rows away from me during my sentencing. My father-in-law and brother-in-law sat across the courtroom from my wife and sister. They distanced themselves from my wife, sister, and me as far as they could. If my wife's father couldn't support his own daughter—what was he doing there? Has media caused us to become so insular to pain and anguish in our own families, that we fail God in His directive to love others as we love ourselves?

Shock, fear, pain, guilt, remorse, pain, and more pain pulsed through every fiber of my being as I was led from the posh, marbled rooms and corridors of a hallowed courthouse, into the dark, inner sanctum of a severely downtrodden dungeon-like prison environment. Society's most vulnerable population resides behind its bond servant, debtor, prison walls. Stop and imagine the eyes of its inhabitants as beaten puppies staring at you from skeletal, abandoned, and frightened bodies behind bars. More vulnerable looking than lost and beaten puppies in a pound waiting to be gassed.

Utterly alone, and thinking not of myself, but for those I have been vanquished from, I continued as the sound of a security door slammed shut behind me for the first time, of my 1,488 day stay. The first words I heard as I entered into my new world were, "Are you a lawyer? Because I need your help." I couldn't see the man that had called out to me for help because his prison-cell was enshrouded by darkness. I found out later that the spiral staircase I had descended that morning in the county prison had not always been a staircase. A *gallows* had once stood in its place. In earlier times, townsfolk had paid to watch hangings in our downtown square, too. Townspeople sometimes wonder why our town struggles to be a vibrant and healthy place. Our past still haunts it. Our county prison is one of the oldest in the country. Our county hired a priest to perform exorcisms—to rid the place of what lingered from its nasty past of hanging and gassing the refuse, culture discharged into it the past 300-plus years.

I am not ashamed to admit that, in my loneliness, I took to sleeping with my Bible, like a child coddles a stuffed animal. On more than one occasion I remember the presence of someone in my bunk when waking from a dream state, only to realize there was no one there, but still feeling the clammy sensation of their presence anyway. Our prison had been built on top of a known Indian tribal burial ground years before schoolhouses and churches became part of our town's infrastructure.

While in county prison, other men had concern for me, and told me that four years was too long to serve in the belly of our prison devoid of windows, education, and worship services. The men told me state facilities would be much better for me because I would be housed in a dormitory like setting with classes and treatment opportunities. I wrote and requested to do my time in state facilities so that I could have access to treatment programs before the sentence contract rescission period expired. They re-sentenced me, but added another four years to my incarceration period. My flat sentence of four years, plus five years probation, was increased to four to eight years—state prison time—plus five years, county probation. For all those who don't know it, that is not legal. Since our country views you from the FED down as state property since birth, it does not matter to them if they make mistakes. To them, you are just a wholly owned subsidiary corporation. You are a bond-servant, or didn't you know?

Nearly every aspect of the incarceration process involves a system of measurement for the purposes of confinement and treatment. In county prison, a pre-sentencing investigation is administered by the pre-trial services' department. Pre-trial solicits written responses from: past employers, doctors that administer psyche evaluations (you should comply), polygraph tests (you should comply), offender assessment board results (you should comply), doctor's reports, therapy session results, and any other interview or evaluation that was ordered and administered by the court. Oh, and the *reason* for sentencing guidelines—if there were none, they'd lock you up for as long as they could, so you could serve as the surety to their bond; sold as a collateralized debt obligation, generated by your default of payment in their courtroom of *charges*.

> Whoever does not obey the law of your God and the
> law of the king, let strict judgment be executed upon
> him, whether death, or corporal punishment, or a fine
> on his goods, or imprisonment.
>
> Ezra 7:26

County "post-sentencing evaluations" were limited to a single questionnaire during intake. In county prison, you are locked down more than twenty out of twenty-four hours. Men literally waste away and are hard pressed to successfully reintegrate back into society, even after a short stay in county jail.

The state prison intake process is significantly more complex and undervalued. After leaving county prison, you'll spend between two to fifteen weeks completing more mental and physical health exams before being moved to your assigned "home jail." The State Department of Corrections (DOC) is all about the type of treatment you'll need, which is dictated by the nature of your offense. The batteries of questions you will answer include hypothetical situations as well as scholastic achievement tests and written versions of your offense. The more honest you are, the better the placement will be in housing you with like-minded individuals. Health and dental concerns are documented through exams and interviews. You will have access to limited dental care, as well as medical treatment, with co-payments required, during the duration of your stay in the state DOC.

Psychological evaluations are given using electronic and written testing. By the time I took the DOC tests, I had completed two other four-hundred-question exams. So I had answered more than 1,200 written questions by the time I had finished the state psyche exams. Don't worry, the bonds they sold in the markets more than paid for everything they provided me. That's how prisoners pay their debt to society, or didn't you know?

Psychological profiles are extremely important to the incarceration process. Psyche profiles indicate how an inmate will cope during their incarceration. Bad coping skills in an inmate put other inmates and staff at risk. Remember that, in the offense cycle—someone who feels offended (like having been incarcerated) may become very bitter over time and act out their anger, especially in the absence of the instillation of good coping skills.

The first re-programming I chose was to read the Holy Bible from cover to cover. Decades ago, every new inmate got a Bible. Now you have to ask for one, and if it's a county jail, they are donated. So supply is limited. In state prison, I was allowed to sing in a ministry team choir, a catholic choir, attend business education classes, and attend worship services, health lectures, computer classes, program treatment, and parenting classes. I worked as a volunteer wheelchair pusher and kept a full-time job in the kitchen. Staying busy and passing your time, gaining insights on how to serve with less, is something that can change a man for the better. I thank God I asked to do my time upstate. If anybody mistakenly believes prisoners should rot in jail, having no access to building good coping skills, then remember *that* when one who has unresolved anger acts out and shocks our nation again. Even national leaders succumb to the offense cycle after they believe their actions are warranted in the aftermath of having been offended by another.

I remember my county pre-trial services contact asking if I had had any thoughts or feelings about hurting myself. I responded, saying that I had a wife and two younger children who were waiting for me to come home to them. And because of them, I had to survive this whole ordeal and return home to them a better husband and father. I owed my family a tremendous debt and that the worst thing I could do was to act out my despondency—further abandoning and inflicting more pain on them. He went on to explain that one of the inmates had hanged himself in his cell that morning, and that he didn't want me to do the same thing. I went on to assure him that I would not and that I would pray for Mr. J.

About a year later, I was assigned a cell with a man who had been in the cell next to Mr. J. the night he hanged himself in county prison. My new cellmate had a tremendous burden, too. His father had committed suicide the day he had been sentenced and he anguished over the fact that he did not stop Mr. J from hanging himself that night. My cellmate explained that Mr. J had had a child sex offense and had been taunted by the inmates and staff to the point he had taken his own life. The inmates had spit and urinated in Mr. J's food outside the bars of his cell before handing his food tray to him regularly. My cellmate was tormented by his own failures to console Mr. J and had also shared with me that he was fully capable of protecting Mr. J because he had protected another inmate—one who had cried out in the middle of the night as *his* cellmate was raping him.

The cycle of offense from unresolved pain and bitterness can be so devastating to individuals that they become *maddened* by wanting to hurt others, back to the point they become offenders, too. Humans can abandon all reason and emulate Lucifer by inflicting pain on others outside of the law. When you become aware of the offense cycle, you begin to see the world as Jesus taught: that we all can become engulfed in pain at one point or another in our lives—acting out our anger. As Jesus said to the throng that wanted to stone the adulteress caught in the act: "Let the one among you who is without sin be the first to throw a stone at her." After each examined their own conscience, one by one, they put their stones on the ground and walked away." Please read John 8:1-9.

Our country's prison system must adapt to allow the convicted to learn why they justified hurting another person and all of society. Which need is greater: to punish the wrong or correct and teach, to help ensure it never happens again? (Correcting and teaching everyone, not just the known offender.) Lawmakers should strive to ensure that everyone leaving prison understands why they made a conscious decision to hurt someone in the past as a way of coping with their pain and resentment. Inmates must be equipped to cope with future pain—without hurting others for the pain and abandonment they feel. Not all prisons are like the state institution where I was. I wish they were, because I think society would benefit through helping more prisoners like the way I've been helped. Budget cuts subsequently removed Bethesda parenting programs from PA prisons. I hope Bethesda Family Services will be recognized by all prison systems for their program's message capability.

I am grateful to him who has strengthened me, Christ Jesus our Lord, because he considered me trustworthy appointing me to the ministry. I was once a blasphemer and a persecutor and an arrogant man, but I have been mercifully treated because I acted out of ignorance in my unbelief. Indeed, the grace of our Lord has been abundant, along with the faith and love that are in Christ Jesus. This saying is trustworthy and deserves full acceptance: Christ Jesus came into the world to save sinners. Of these I am the foremost. But for that reason I was mercifully treated, so that in me, as the foremost, Christ Jesus might display all his patience as an example for those who would come to believe in him for everlasting life. To the king of ages, incorruptible, invisible, the only God, honor and glory forever and ever! Amen.

1 Timothy 1:12-17

namely, God was reconciling the world to himself in Christ, not counting their trespasses against them and entrusting to us the message of reconciliation. So we are ambassadors for Christ, as if God were appealing through us. We implore you on behalf of Christ, be reconciled to God. For our sake he made him to be sin who did not know sin, so that we might become the righteousness of God in him.

2 Corinthians 5:19-21

To love and when rejected; learn to forgive, make new agreements, let go and move beyond.

CHAPTER SEVEN

Love Conquers Selfishness

- Do you truly desire to be so different from your heavenly Father?

- Do you feel known, understood, appreciated, respected and included?

- Do you feel loved, unconditionally, for the rest of eternity?

- Do you want others in your life to feel completely and unconditionally loved by you?

- Do you want others to feel known, understood, appreciated, respected and included by you?

From the time we lost our intimacy with our tender Father in the garden of Eden, His love continues to connect with us through His chosen representatives by His Holy Spirit. Miraculously, everyone who connects with His love wants everyone else to experience it.

How would you react if the one you loved wanted to leave you?

Out of respect and love, would you let them live a life separated from you? Could you *really* believe that you put *them* before yourself if you are incapable of giving what they desire most? Giving, even if it meant separating from them *forever*? There are two instinctive responses—fight or flight. But our heavenly Father teaches us a third, through His Son Jesus: *give.*

By giving, there is a reduction of the escalation of anger, pain, and guilt in relationship with others for the rest of your life. After all, is that not the very relationship we have received all along from our tender heavenly Father? Has He not given beyond measure of time and material? Loving us through eternity even when we fail to Love Him!!

> For if their rejection is the reconciliation of the world,
> what will their acceptance be but life from the dead?
>
> Romans 11:15

Perfection is man's ideological concept.

To fail is only human…*to forgive is truly divine.*

Perseverance teaches us there are seasons to our lives, just as there are seasons to time.

The Lord's prayer is to teach everyone how to honor and pray to our Father in heaven:

> Teaching about prayer. When you pray, do not be like the hypocrites, who love to stand and pray in the synagogues and on street corners so that others may see them. Amen, I say to you, they have received their reward. But when you pray, go to your inner room, close the door, and pray to your Father in secret. And your Father who sees in secret will repay you. In praying, do not babble like the pagans, who think that they will be heard because of their many words. Do not be like them. Your Father knows what you need before you ask him. The Lord's Prayer.

This is how you are to pray: Our Father in heaven, hallowed be your name, your kingdom come, your will be done, on earth as in heaven. Give us today our daily bread; and forgive us our debts, as we forgive our debtors; and do not subject us to the final test, but deliver us from the evil one. If you forgive others their transgressions, your heavenly Father will forgive you. But if you do not forgive others, neither will your Father forgive your transgressions.

Matthew 6:5-15

Obstinately, persisting in our self-interests, choosing to be separated from our Father's love, and holding back forgiveness from any of His children is what we must all turn away from. Refrain from perpetuating the adversary's lie and accept the correction program as a gift from our heavenly Father through His only son, and Spirit of truth.

What must you forgive of someone else who has failed you before you leave this life? Do you plan to face Jesus who died for you whilst stuck in your inability to be merciful to those who need your forgiveness the most?

> God's irrevocable call: I do not want you to be unaware of this mystery, brothers, so that you will not become wise in your own estimation: a hardening has come upon Israel in part, until the full number of the Gentiles comes in, and thus all Israel will be saved, as it is written: The deliverer will come out of Zion; he will turn away ungodliness from Jacob; and this is my covenant with them, when I take away their sins. In respect to the gospel, they are enemies on your account; but in respect to election, they are beloved because of the patriarchs. For the gifts and the call of God are irrevocable. Triumph of God's Mercy: Just as you once disobeyed God but have now received mercy because

of their disobedience, so they have now disobeyed in order that, by virtue of the mercy shown to you, they too may (now) receive mercy. For God delivered all to disobedience, that he might have mercy upon all.

Romans 11:25-32

The Way of Love. But I shall show you a still more excellent way. If I speak in human and angelic tongues but do not have love, I am a resounding gong or a clashing cymbal. And if I have the gift of prophecy and comprehend all mysteries and all knowledge; if I have all faith so as to move mountains but do not have love, I am nothing. If I give away everything I own, and if I hand my body over so that I may boast but do not have love, I gain nothing. Love is patient, love is kind. It is not jealous, (love) is not pompous, it is not inflated, it is not rude, it does not seek its own interests, it is not quick tempered, it does not brood over injury, it does not rejoice over wrongdoing but rejoices with the truth. It bears all things, believes all things, hopes all things, endures all things. Love never fails. If there are prophecies, they will be brought to nothing; if tongues, they will cease; if knowledge, it will be brought to nothing. For we know partially and we prophesy partially, but when the perfect comes, the partial will pass away. When I was a child, I used to talk as a child, think as a child, reason as a child. When I became a man, I put aside childish things. At present we see indistinctly, as in a mirror, but then face to face. At present I know partially, then I shall know fully, as I am fully known. So faith, hope, love remain, these three; but the greatest of these is love.

1 Corinthians 13

And even when you were dead (in) transgressions and the uncircumcision of your flesh, he brought you to life along with him, having forgiven us all our transgressions; obliterating the bond against us, with its legal claims, which was opposed to us, he also removed it from our midst, nailing it to the cross; despoiling the principalities and the powers, he made a public spectacle of them, leading them away in triumph by it.

Colossians 2:13-15

Should you not have had pity on your fellow servant, I had pity on you? Then in anger his master handed him over to the torturers until he should pay back the whole debt. So will my heavenly Father do to you, unless each of you forgives his brother from his heart.

Matthew 18:33-35

Throughout your life, Christ's teaching has been at work, regardless of your knowledge of it. Who do you choose not to forgive? What is the price you pay for it?

I am growing, I am stronger, and I love more purely, and appreciate life more fully. I appreciate you for allowing me to share my story. I hope you feel an increase of being known, understood, appreciated, respected and included through this *our time together*. My Prayers are answered because our time spent together helps make my time away from my family—productive, enriching, and fulfilling; producing good from bad. Life is bitter sweet for both you and I.

All praise, honor, and glory be to our sweet and patient Father in heaven.

Love,

Your brother in Christ; once a prisoner of disobedience; set free by the love of God,

Mark-Hour/ *Without Prejudice*

He came to what was his own, but his own people did not accept him.

John 1:11

And now these three remain: faith, hope, and love. But the greatest of these is love.

1 Corinthians 13:13

CHAPTER EIGHT

The Take Away

e are made in the image of God. When we conceive of something (God the Father) and believe in it (God the Holy Spirit) then we achieve it (God the Son in whom all things are made).

The pain and anger I have focused on with you is *that* pain which causes you to mask your emotional vulnerabilities from others. Have you put on your *game face* while being crushed on the inside by deep emotional hurt? Coping with pain for each individual is different. The outcome of changing *who* you are is almost always the same. You withhold your trust until your new plan's criteria is met. You shield your inner child and strive to integrate solutions to the problems as you perceive them. Anger and resentment build as new methods of protecting and controlling fail. For me, I hid my fears from others, used external stuff, people, places and things, while all along I *feared* loss.

If you have not already, my challenge to you is to read *every word* and scripture within as if *you* have abandoned your inner child, God's creation. That *you* are responsible for the breach in relationships you suffer from because you *think* your solutions are the best ones that fit your needs to heal and retain relationship with others. Please read and digest every word keeping in mind that deep down inside *you starve* for connection with others.

Now, remembering that child who yearns for pure love, believe that God suffers in silence watching his children afflict one another. The solution we share in common with God is: To love and when rejected; learn to forgive, make new agreements, let go and move beyond.

When emotions do fly, and anger abounds, "filter your thoughts" remembering that anger *aimed* at you reflects how important you are to the other person. The more "reactive" the anger, the more the other person is expressing they feel *you* don't care about or understand what is important to them.

It has been said that you hurt the ones you love. A better comprehension is: the ones who love you will tell you that you hurt them by expressing their anger and pain. Do not become defensive when someone expresses hurt and pain. You must try to look beyond *their* offensive behavior realizing they are acting-out an expression of how much you affected them. Tell them that you appreciate them trusting you and telling you how *they* feel. That you really appreciate them telling you how important you are to them and that you are sorry *you* hurt *them*. You must reconcile with them and tell them you are truly sorry and want to make up with them.

Only God could perceive our *affliction* correctly. Only Jesus could complete life without hurting anyone or anything, not even the shaft of a bruised reed. Read Isaiah 42: 1-9.

The title for this work is: God's Kingdom 13:13 The Secret Pain. Obviously tying it all back to God's perfect love described in 1 Corinthians 13.

Through treatment programs inside and outside of prison, I have learned about thinking errors, pretend norms, and the cycle of offense, relationship boundaries, intimacy, forgiveness, healing, reconciliation and *letting go*. Rather than impose everything I learned on you, I thought

I'd produce a work that would serve as a guide to bring you through a process, allowing God's word and history along with my experiences to lead you to what *you* need to heal, with others.

My prayer is that through your hard work, you will "filter" what you say, hear and do. Align your soul with our heavenly Father and His love. Stop acting like the father of this world who justifies hurting you and everyone else. Let go and let God in your life. And, remember; Lucifer wants *you* to hold onto your past pain and anger. Lucifer wants you to focus on your pain, ignore God's love and go down into the abyss with him in the end.

You owe an insurmountable debt, which you are incapable of paying. Read Matthew 18:21-35. Jesus taught Peter to forgive 77 times 7 when offended by another. Read Matthew 18:15-20.

God's *gift* is his spirit of discernment; you are aware of the corruption and gain greater control over your soul and are equipped to model a more perfect love. Better than any tithe or prayer is fulfilling the Law as Christ did: to love God with your entire mind, heart and actions and to love others as you love yourself.

How much social benefit will come from everyone acting-out less often towards others when they feel justified? In monetary affairs reducing: tax evasion, embezzlement and insurance fraud, just to name a few. If everyone could perceive, filter, and love with more clarity a little more often, *heaven* will truly reside on earth, for *the law* will finally be comprehended and modeled after the Alpha and Omega, Jesus Christ our Lord and Savior.

I hope that you will think before you react and remember; love does not fail. Love also knows when to *give in* to the demands of another, and let go. Love does not hold onto past hurts.

In the past, I stuffed my pain and at times exploded with dire consequences. Please share your *fear* and your courage with equal emphasis with loved ones. It is amazing how much trust and connection is built as a result.

God the Father created us in His image. We starve to be known, understood, appreciated, respected and included while in relationship with others who are important to us. That is due to the fact that God wants *us* to know Him, understand Him, appreciate Him, respect Him and include Him. He does not demand all our time, understanding, or appreciation... He understands we are limited in our abilities to comprehend, be grateful and include Him in our plans. He just wants us to be honest and remember Him and talk with Him as a friend. He does not expect perfection; He knows us, understands us, appreciates us, respects us and includes us. He gave us Jesus to fulfill what we were unable to because of *our corrupted minds-- our knowledge of both good and evil.* God draws us to Him through the pain we experience and when we understand that fact, we are then released from perfectionism and reborn into a state of *grace.* We are called to extend that grace to others who fall short of fulfilling what we desire of them, too. And so, we pay the grace given us forward. That is true Christianity.

Way back in 1982 I stayed overnight quite often with Suzanne, who lived with her mother and brother. She had broken up with me after months of being in relationship with her and decided to date Patrick over the Christmas holidays. I did not take the break-up well. Being rejected I took to consoling myself with friends, alcohol and more. The night of the first day January 1983 I was with friends in a barn playing the drinking game *quarters* with hard-mixed-liquors instead of just beer. In a short period of time we had consumed more than several shots each of alcohol. By 11:45 pm we separated and went home. I had dropped John off at his parents home and ended up passing out behind the wheel of a V8 Mustang, bouncing it off a tree about 20 feet in the air before it landed. I found myself in a tunnel with a bright light at the end and feeling a wonderful sense of being there before, deja'vu multiplied 20x strong and feeling like I was home again and belonged there and not where I had been prior. Home, a strong sense of belonging and Love beyond any feeling of love or belonging permeated my being. Out of the light appeared Mary and she spoke with me telling me that I could not stay. I begged her not to make me go back. She said it was not my time and I could not stay. She told me I had work to do. Instantly I was back in my body, bleeding profusely. I was then met by a neighbor of the household I crashed in the front yard of. I was then sent to the hospital where they operated on me for 5 hours. I was 20 years old when that occurred and did not speak of my out of body experience short of a few close relatives and friends literally for decades. I share this experience often now because, even though I actually saw the gates of heaven at 20, I went on in life to make several additional life changing decisions that impacted my life and family very negatively. I have also made extremely good decisions to be fair to myself. My point is, even though I had this experience early in my life, I went on to live a human pain filled life. God knows it all, from start to finish. He knows you, too. Please remember, you were literally stolen from your Heavenly Father in the Garden of Eden when Adam and Eve fell prey to the enemy's trickery, corrupting our minds with the knowledge of both good and evil. God has done everything He could do to bring you home to Him. Please do not deny Him, for your own sake and eternity in Heaven where you belong, too. Please realize, there are many YouTube video testimonies of folk who have gone down into the pit, as well as, gone to the gates of Heaven and beyond, some even having met Jesus, too.

B. L. U. E.

Being Loved Unconditionally Eternally
By Mark Hour

Blue is the color of my heart
suffocated by loneliness, being so far
from you.

Blue is the color of endless skies
permeating my memory, straining to maintain
all our enchanted moments spent together;
when it seamed even the angels and all onlookers
gazed in wistful longing to be part of *us*
when our time was still new.

Blue is the color of eyes
that long to reflect back all
the intense desire so long kept
from who it rightfully belongs to.

Blue is the color of my blessed mother's
attire; who knows all the pain and sorrow
this world so easily can afflict,
and, mistakenly pursue.

Blue is the wonder of my mind
that is no longer cavalier.

Blue is the wonder of all this world
caught up in my heart
when I think of you.

Blue is being loved unconditionally eternally;
which is all I have to give,
and want with you.
Whenever we are going to be,
whatever we need to do,
it's not about control,
but what love dictates we do.

Love exists, so wisdom does too.

Is It Love or Mental Illness?
They're Closer Than You Think

Originally featured in the *Wall Street Journal*
February 13, 2007, Health Journal
By Tara Parker Pope
Please go to:
http://online.wsj.com/article/SB117131067930406235.html#

No Easy Answers

Question: How would you feel if children were being *prosecuted* using the same statutes you thought lawmakers wrote to *protect* children?

To learn more about Sexual Crimes, and useful solutions that need to be increased for the protection of men, women, and children, please go to: www.hrw.org. Or, paste in your browser: http://www.hrw.org/en/reports/2007/09/11/no-easy-answers-0

No Easy Answers
September 2007 Volume 19. No.4G
By the United Nations
Human Rights Watch

A Nation of Innkeepers
By a Friend—Melvin S.

In Florida, recently, the only "approved home plan" for five paroled sex offenders was under an overpass. It reminded me of a story handed down to us long ago.

A man and his very pregnant wife sought food and lodging and warmth, but were turned away by innkeeper after innkeeper. The baby was born with only straw and animals to shelter him from the elements. While the infant never posed a danger to society, the government nevertheless cited his "future dangerousness" and branded him a targeted class and a threat to public safety. The government's political agenda forced his family to leave their community and loved ones, and take refuge in Egypt.

The baby grew up aware of his humble beginnings as an outcast. And so he devoted his entire life to befriending the lowest of the low— lepers, tax collectors, sex offenders, and murderers. He once told a story about another outcast, a Samaritan, who exemplified the best of humanity while embarrassing the self-righteous.

Fanned by public hysteria, authorities told lies in order to condemn one who chose to associate with those despised by society. The politicos succeeded, and his earthly reward was a death sentence, reserved for those convicted of the most heinous crimes.

With his final breath, he still reached out in forgiveness and mercy to a fellow convict who was being executed with him.

Today, there is a conspicuous scarcity of those who claim to profess forgiveness and mercy—churches, shelters, agencies, charities—who are willing to reach out to those outcasts under the bridge, and all others who are similarly situated.

Yet, those ostracized by society can take comfort from the baby born centuries ago, who grew up to bring hope and encouragement to his fellow prisoners and outcasts, and know that they have an Advocate and "Friend in high places." Too bad about the innkeepers.

—By Melvin S.

A Nation of Innkeepers was originally featured in Graterfriends;

PA Prison Society publication.

Founded in 1787, the Pennsylvania Prison Society is a social justice organization that advocates on behalf of prisoners, formerly incarcerated individuals and their families. Headquartered in Philadelphia, the Prison Society offers direct services and official prison visitation through a network of statewide chapters.

http://www.prisonsociety.org/about/index.shtml

(Accessed 03/21/2010)

Call:
215.564.6005 Extension 106

E-Mail:
Catherine Wise
Director of Development and Communications

Write:
The Pennsylvania Prison Society
245 North Broad Street
Suite 300
Philadelphia, PA 19107

Acknowledgments

http://www.bfsf.org (Accessed 03/21/2010)

Bethesda Family Services Foundation

88 Bull Run Crossing, Suite 1
Lewisburg, PA 17837
(570) 523-0605
Fax: (570) 523-0676
Parenting Skills Seminars

Bethesda also offers Parenting Skills Seminars, which take participants through our "Four Steps to Emotional Healing." Parenting Skills Seminars cover topics such as:

- Simple and effective parenting skills
- Restorative discipline
- Truth-based communication skills
- Strengthening relationships through intimacy development
- Anger dissolution and reconciliation

All parenting skills are achieved through reconciliation and restoration. Bethesda provides parents with methods of converting parent anger into constructive action through practical instruction of our "3 D's and 2 P's" of parental authority. These methods are simple to learn but profound in impact.

Original Cover Art/Painting
by Ingrid Heil
https://www.ingridabledesign.biz/index.html

http://www.hrw.org/en/reports/2007/09/11/no-easy-answers-0

"No Easy Answers" September 2007 Volume 19. No.4G
By the United Nations

Human Rights Watch Mission Statement: Human Rights Watch is dedicated to protecting the human rights of people around the world. We stand with victims and activists to prevent discrimination, to uphold political freedom, to protect people from inhumane conduct in wartime, and to bring offenders to justice. We investigate and expose human rights violations and hold abusers accountable. We challenge governments and those who hold power to end abusive practices and respect international human rights law. We enlist the public and the international community to support the cause of human rights for all.

Saint Joseph Giant Type Edition of
The New American Bible
Catholic Book Publishing
New York, New York
Copyright 1992, 1990

Anxiety, fear, ADDHD and other symptoms of fear
are reduced by reading and consuming Gods Word

Note: This space can be used to write answers posed by questions you
will encounter on pages within.

_____

_____

_____

_____

_____

_____

_____

_____

_____

_____

_____

_____

_____

_____

_____

_____

_____

_____